Solving the Social Media Puzzle: 7 Simple Steps to Planning a Social Media Marketing Strategy for Your Business

Companion Workbook v. 1

Copyright 2012 by Kathryn Rose and Apryl Parcher. All rights reserved. First edition 2012. Published in the United States of America.

Table of Contents

Introduction

Is this you?

- You have heard all the hype about having a presence on social media but you don't know where to begin.
- You are starting a business or have a business and are looking to take it to the next level and need some help organizing your strategies.
- You have a presence on social media sites but have not seen the results you desire.
- You are a busy professional and don't have time to "fool around" on Facebook and Twitter.
- You want actionable advice on how to use these newer online tools to get more visibility and make more money.
- You want to know how to measure your results using free tools.

Well, if any of these are even CLOSE to being you, it's time to pull back the veil. Social media is not a big mystery—social media is a wonderful addition to your marketing mix. If used properly, it's a tool that can bring awareness, drive traffic and profits to your business, and more importantly, build a community of loyal fans and followers.

Let's get started building a successful, workable and easy to use plan for your social media marketing!

This workbook is meant to complement the book *Solving the Social Media Puzzle: 7 Simple Steps to Planning a Social Media Marketing Strategy for Your Business*. If you have not read the book, we suggest you start there and use the exercises in this workbook to give you more information and get you started quickly.

Lesson 1: Developing Your Target Market

1.1.1 Written Exercise: Who Does Your Product Serve?

To begin visualizing a true picture of the types of people—creating "personas" like the ones we gave you in the book-- you should be targeting for your marketing messages, consider these questions:

1. What problem does my product or service solve; what gap does it fill?

2. Who does my product or service serve?

Think about those people you want to attract. Even if you have a business-to-business target, *people* buy products, not businesses, so this exercise is still worth completing. Who is most likely to be interested in what you have to offer?

Don't say "everybody" or women or men or moms or dads in general. There are probably certain groups of market segments that will be more likely to purchase your product but try and get specific if you can. It's important to identify such segments, whether you're doing consumer, retail or business-to-business marketing, so that you can focus your marketing efforts and dollars on those most likely to generate a profitable return.

Write your answers on the next page:

1. What problem does my product or service solve; what gap does it fill?

_____

_____

_____

_____

_____

_____

2. Who does my product or service serve?

_____

_____

_____

_____

1.1.2 Written Exercise: Broad Market Targeting

Now that you've identified who your product serves, let's start on the path to getting to the heart of your target market by defining your market broadly using demographics.

According to Business Dictionary.com demographics is defined as:

> Socioeconomic characteristics of a population expressed statistically, such as age, sex, education level, income level, marital status, occupation, religion, birth rate, death rate, average size of a family, average age at marriage.

Think carefully for a moment about who is purchasing your product currently or who you think your product will serve based upon the exercise you completed previously (visualize them, maybe you know them personally or can look up their profiles on social networks) and answer the following questions:

What is the general age?

Gender?   _____

Education level?   _____

Income level?   _____

Marital Status?   _____

Occupation?   _____

Religion?   _____

Do they have children? How many children and at what stage of life (infants, toddlers, teens, etc.)? _____

_____

1.1.3 Written Exercise: Target market definition using Psychographics

While demographics describe the general profile of a particular segment of the market, psychographics refer to attitudes, lifestyles and other traits people exhibit in their approach to life. Put psychographic traits together with demographic traits and you're one step closer to determining who your target market is:

Once again, close your eyes and visualize the person. What are they doing, reading watching? You can go to brick and mortar version of your similar business and just observe. Go to the nearest bookstore and observe those who would fit your general demographic to get this information or use your best guess based upon your experience. Again, using the social networks could be key; go to the Facebook profile of your ideal customer and click on the "about" under their cover photo. If they allow it through privacy settings you can see who their friends are, what pages they've liked and so on. If that person has their profile locked down go to the next and the next until you find some that offer the information. Go to Twitter and see what their bio says and see what they're tweeting about, similarly with Linkedin, etc.

Now, write down the following psychographic characteristics of your buyer:

Occupation: _____

Social Class: _____

Hobbies: _____

_____

_____

TV shows they may watch: _____

_____

_____

Newspapers they may read: _____

_____

_____

Magazines they may subscribe to: _____

_____

_____

Restaurants they may enjoy: _____

_____

_____

Movies they may watch: _____

_____

_____

Personality traits: _____

_____

_____

Risk takers vs. conservative?   _____

Technology users/adaptors?   _____

Smartphone users?   _____

What motivates them to buy your product? Is it for social status? To make more revenue? To make them feel good about themselves? Make someone else feel better?

_____

_____

_____

_____

1.1.4 Written Exercise: Create a Survey

One of the things we recommend in the book is to survey either your current customers or those you feel should be part of your target audience and get some information from them directly. When you do surveys, it's best to keep them short. One of the best ways we've found to get people to respond to surveys is to give something away in exchange for them answering the survey. We've actually had people email and thank us for giving them the opportunity to fill out a survey where we were doing a drawing of participants and giving away a $100 gift card. $100 is not that much to give away if you get lots of information that will make your product or service better.

Best Practices for Designing a Survey

1. **Define your objectives.** What kind of information do you need? In this case, you are simply trying to get a clear picture of your target market. Questions should be formulated to find out information on the demographics and psychographics of your client base. Also keep in mind that you will want to find out the "pain" points for your clients.
2. **Who is the target of the survey?** You can use one survey for current customers and one for prospects.
3. **Creating Questions:** Make sure questions are clear and concise. Try to do a mix of closed and open-ended questions. For example, be careful not to use any industry jargon or acronyms. Think through the length of the survey carefully. People don't like to answer lots of questions. In some cases it could depend on what the give-away is. For example, if you have no give-away, don't ask more than ten questions. If you

are doing a drawing for a gift card, iPad, etc. you can probably get away with a longer survey. No more than 25 questions, it should not be longer than 15 minutes to complete.
4. **Do a simple marketing plan for your survey.** When are you going to send it? How are you going to distribute it?

To get you started, here are some sample survey questions:

(Note: You may or may not need all of them to create your personas. For example, religious affiliation may not be a mandatory field but if you include it, it could clue you in on some of the psychographic and cultural things that may help you to formulate your personas. It is completely up to you).

Sample General Survey Questions:

1) Are you Male or Female?

Male   Female

2) What is your age? (Be sure not to overlap choices)

Select one...   18-21   22-25   26-30   31-40   41-50   51-60   61 or over

3) What is the highest level of education you have completed?

Select one...   Less than High School   High School/GED   Some College   2-Year College Degree(Associates)   4-Year College Degree(BA,BS)   Master's Degree   Doctoral Degree Professional Degree(MD,JD)

4) What are your income and your total household income? (You may or may not want to give them the option to "opt out" of this question.)

Your income: Select one... Less than $10,000 $10,000-$19,999 $20,000-$29,999 $30,000-$39,999 $40,000-$49,999 $50,000-$59,999 $60,000-$69,999 $70,000-$79,999 $80,000-$89,999 $90,000-$99,999 $100,000-$149,000 More than $150,000 Prefer not to answer

Total household: Select one... Less than $10,000 $10,000-$19,999 $20,000-$29,999 $30,000-$39,999 $40,000-$49,999 $50,000-$59,999 $60,000-$69,999 $70,000-$79,999 $80,000-$89,999 $90,000-$99,999 $100,000-$149,000 More than $150,000

5) What is your current marital status?

Single, Never Married

Married

Separated

Divorced

Widowed

6) What is your religious affiliation?

Protestant Christian

Roman Catholic

Evangelical Christian

Jewish

Muslim

Hindu

Buddhist

Other:

7) What is your race?

Select one...   White   African-American   Hispanic   Asian-Pacific Islander   Native American

8) Do you have children? Yes/No

If yes, how many?

What are their ages?

9) What interests you in your free time?

10) What events have you participated in during the past month?

11) What topics do you enjoy reading about?

12) What television shows do you watch on a regular basis?

13) What newspapers/magazines do you read regularly?

14) How would you best describe your personality? (May want to give examples.)

15) How frequently do you visit our store/website?

16) What motivated you to choose our store today?

17) What do you normally purchase at our store/website?

18) How much do you typically spend at our store/website?

19) What other stores like ours do you like to visit?

20) Where did you hear about our store/website/products?

If you would like to be included in the drawing for the

$100 gift card please fill out the following information:

Name, email, twitter handle, Facebook page URL

Example of a Business Website Evaluation

1) For which of the following reasons have you visited our website? (Check all that apply)

Product Information

Product Support

Sales Information

Company Information

Company/Department Contact

Employment Opportunities

Other:

2) Please grade the overall content of our website.

NOTE: Use the choices, Excellent, Good, Average, Poor, Very Poor, Undecided (or don't know) for each of these questions unless otherwise noted

3) Please grade the ease of navigation of our website.

4) Please grade the overall look of our website.

5) The information on the website is clearly written and easy to understand.

6) The content of the website is up-to-date.

7) The information on the website met my needs.

8) The layout of the website is well-organized and clear.

9) The links on the website are current and working.

10) How does our website compare to similar websites you have visited?

Example of an E-Store Evaluation

1) How did you learn about our online store?

Friend or Relative

Web Search Engine

Banner Ad

Magazine

Web-Based Article

E-Mail

Pop-Up Ad

Other:

2) What was the MAIN reason you visited our online store?

Browsing

Particular Item

Comparison of Prices

Other:

3) How easy was it to navigate the web site?

NOTE: use the choices: Very Easy, Somewhat Easy, Easy, Somewhat Difficult, Very Difficult, for each of these questions unless otherwise noted.

4) How easy was it to find a particular item you were looking for?

5) How easy was it to browse our inventory?

6) Did you make a purchase from our online store?

 Yes

 No (skip to question 18)

7) Was this a personal purchase for you, a gift, a company purchase, or something else?

 Personal

 Gift

 Company Purchase

 Other:

8) How easy was it to move items into your shopping cart? (Use choices from Question 3.)

9) How easy was it to remove items from your shopping cart? (Use choices from Question 3.)

10) How easy was it to modify items in your shopping cart? For instance to change quantity, color, size, etc. (use choices from question 3)

11) How easy was it to resume shopping after placing items in your shopping cart? (Use choices from Question 3.)

12) How did you pay for your purchase?

Credit Card Online

Credit Card by Phone

Check by Mail

Check by Phone

Company Purchase Order

C.O.D.

Other:

13) How satisfied were you with the available shipping options? (Use choices from Question 3.)

14) Was your order complete when you received it?

Yes

No

15) Did you return any items you purchased from our online store?

Yes

No

16) What was the main reason for your return?

Wrong Size

Wrong Color

Not What I Ordered

Damaged

Not Satisfied with Item

Other:

17) How satisfied were you with the return process? (Use choices from Question 3.)

18) What was the MAIN reason you did not make a purchase from our online store?

Price

Availability of Item

Shipping Options

Selection

Difficulty Navigating Site

Payment Options

Other:

19) Overall, how satisfied were you with your shopping experience at our online store? (Use choices from Question 3.)

20) Do you think you will shop at our online store again?

Yes

No

21) What, if anything, can we do to improve your experience at our online store?

NOTE: Be sure to add open-ended questions that pertain to their attitudes toward your brand or store. You can get information you didn't anticipate.

You don't need a huge sampling to get you on the right path to determining your target market. Many political polls are based on small samples. Get as many as you can, it's better than nothing!

In the space below, and the next page, write down questions for your survey:

_____

_____

_____

_____

_____

_____

_____

1.1.5 Written Exercise: Creating a Phone Survey

In the book we also recommended that you make a list of your top 20-50 customers, fans, followers and try to contact them by phone to ask specific questions. You can design an "insiders club" or something to reward these individuals for their assistance. In the case of a phone survey you will want to ask more open-ended questions. We recommend recording the calls if possible. Be sure to let the person know you are recording the call. It's tough to take notes and speak at the same time. One of our favorite free sites is http://www.freeconferencecalling.com; it offers a way to record calls.

Like the written survey, you want to make sure you don't take up too much of their time, or for longer surveys, give them something worth giving up 15-30 minutes. Many times the calls will go over that time, but you want to make sure the person knows that your questions will take no more than 30 minutes. On the phone, you can ask more open-ended questions like: "What problem are you trying to solve with our solution?" or "Why did you choose us over the competition?"

We also recommend that you write out your telephone script, including your introduction, so you have something to look at. Write out one script for live calls (where you actually reach someone,) and another for having to leave messages. Here's a sample live call introduction using an online ski retailer as an example:

Hi Joe, this is Allen from BIG AIR SKI SHOP.

Got a quick favor to ask—You're one of our best customers, and I'd like to ask you a few questions to help us improve the shop… shouldn't take more than 15-20 minutes, and I'd love to send you a thank-you gift for helping us out—a $20 gift card. Now I know you're busy, so feel free to say no if you're jammed up…

If YES: That's Great! Thanks so much Joe—we really appreciate it. When's a good time to set up our call— or do you have a few minutes right now?

If NO: That's perfectly ok, Joe—not a problem—you take it easy ok?

With your top customers in mind determine a good thank-you gift that would be of value to your customer, and write out an introductory script for your survey call. Don't forget to write out "NO and YES" scripts. As you go through these calls, you'll eventually get comfortable with the wording and won't have to look at your script, but this really helps focus your thoughts when you're on the phone.

Some sample phone survey questions:

Here are some sample phone survey questions for our ski retailer:

Thank you for agreeing to participate (name), I'm going to start by asking some general questions about you. Feel free to skip any questions you are not comfortable with, and then I'll ask specific questions about our ski shop:

What is your age (give ranges)?

What is your income (give ranges – keep in mind they will probably say they make more than they do)?

What is your marital status?

Do you have children? How many? What are their ages?

Where do you live (general geographic region)?

What are your favorite TV Shows?

Magazines/Newspapers?

What type of music do you listen to?

Besides skiing what would you say your hobbies are?

What's your favorite winter sport, and how would you describe your level of expertise?

How did you find out about us before you started doing business with us?

What problems were you having that we helped you solve?

Would you rather shop in the store or do you prefer online shopping? Why?

Have you dealt with our customer service department on an issue?
How could we have improved our service to you?

What would you say is our greatest strength as a ski shop?

What would you say is our greatest weakness?

It's your turn: Write out a list of questions for your business that would help you better identify your target market and their needs (including the demographic questions as well as the more open-ended ones like those listed above).

_____

_____

_____

_____

_____

_____

_____

_____

1.1.6 Written Exercise: Persona Creation

Now that you've done your homework, it's time to give your market a face, name and write down the characteristics of each. You will be creating your top three personas. Just like the example we gave you in the book. Remember Multitasker Mike? Here's an example to get you started:

Here's our example for Multitasker Mike (CTO)

Name: Multitasker Mike

Characteristics:

Male, age 45

Income level: $150,000

Married

Kids/No Kids: 2 (ages 12 and 15)

TV Shows: Fox News, CNN, Dirty Jobs, Boss, How it's Made

Pain points (How does your product solve their problem? How does it serve them?) Needs to disprove cost center assumptions of peers/superiors; Limited amount of time; suspicious of "quick fix" solutions—needs proof.

Books/magazines/newspapers they read: Fortune, Money, Smart Computing, CIO, Technology Review

Now it's your turn: Use Google images (http://images.google.com/) to find someone that looks the part. Take a screen shot and paste them into this document

Persona #1

Name: _____

Characteristics (attitude, lifestyle, traits):

_____

Put a face picture here

_____

Male/Female: _____

Income level: _____

Married/Single: _____

Kids/No Kids: _____

TV Shows: _____

_____

Books/magazines/newspapers they read: _____

_____

Pain points (How does your product solve their problem? How does it serve them?): _____

_____

Now it's your turn: Persona #2

Persona #1

Name: _____

Characteristics (attitude, lifestyle, traits):

_____

| Put a face picture here |

_____

Male/Female: _____

Income level: _____

Married/Single: _____

Kids/No Kids: _____

TV Shows: _____

_____

Books/magazines/newspapers they read: _____

_____

Pain points (How does your product solve their problem? How does it serve them?): _____

_____

_____

The main persona

Now you need to choose the main persona you will agree to create content for over the next 60 days. To keep you focused print our cut out the persona from the workbook and hang it on the wall of your office.

Lesson 2: Goals

2.1.1. Written Exercise: Choosing your goals

Here are the main reasons businesses use social networks;

1. **Brand awareness:** Simply put, you want as many people as possible to know about you, your brand and your products or services.

2. **Customer service:** You want a way to communicate better or in real time with your customers.

3. **Increasing website or blog traffic:** You have great content but you want more people to read it.

4. **Client acquisition:** You already have a well-known brand and have put together an active online community and now you're ready to start driving business through social networking.

Choose your number one and two and write the reasons below:

1. _____

_____

_____

2. _____

_____

_____

Lesson 3: Get your blog together

In the book we refer to the blog as the "hub" of all online activity:

So, no matter what your persona and goals, you must lay the foundation that will provide content for all of your online activities.

3.1.1 Written Exercise: Themes for Your Blog

One of the ways we suggest you get blog content is by using "themes." Developing themes like "Holiday" or "Spring" will help you create content.

Use the space below to write out 12 months of themes for your blog posts:

January   _____

February   _____

March   _____

April   _____

May   _____

June   _____

July   _____

August   _____

September   _____

October   _____

November   _____

December   _____

3.1.2 Written Exercise: Write out specific post topics

One of the ways we suggested to find out blog topics for your audience is to use the Google Keyword Tool (http://googlekeywordtool.com). Type in the main keywords you think your market would use to find you online. For example with a search on the keyword tool "Social Media," you will see things like "What is social media" "How to use social media." etc. That will give you a good start. Now, go to the bonus "Top 50 Blog Ideas" we gave you with the book, use it to brainstorm 12 specific blog post ideas using the space below that correspond to the themes you wrote in the last exercise(here's the download link for the bonus: http://solvingthesocialmediapuzzle.com/hg52-62a980T5/Top-50-blog-ideas.zip):

1. _____

2. _____

3. _____

4. _____

5. _____

6. _____

7. _____

8. _____

9. _____

10. _____

11. _____

12. _____

3.1.3 Written Exercise: Use a "Spinoff Diagram"

One of the other ways we suggested coming up with additional blog ideas is to use a "spinoff" diagram. A spinoff diagram is a big circle with the main blog title the middle and related topics in the smaller circles. Here is the example from the book using a ski shop as an example:

Your turn: Using the themes and the top 50 blog ideas, now create your own "spinoff" diagrams so you have 24 posts, 2 per month:

Diagram 1:

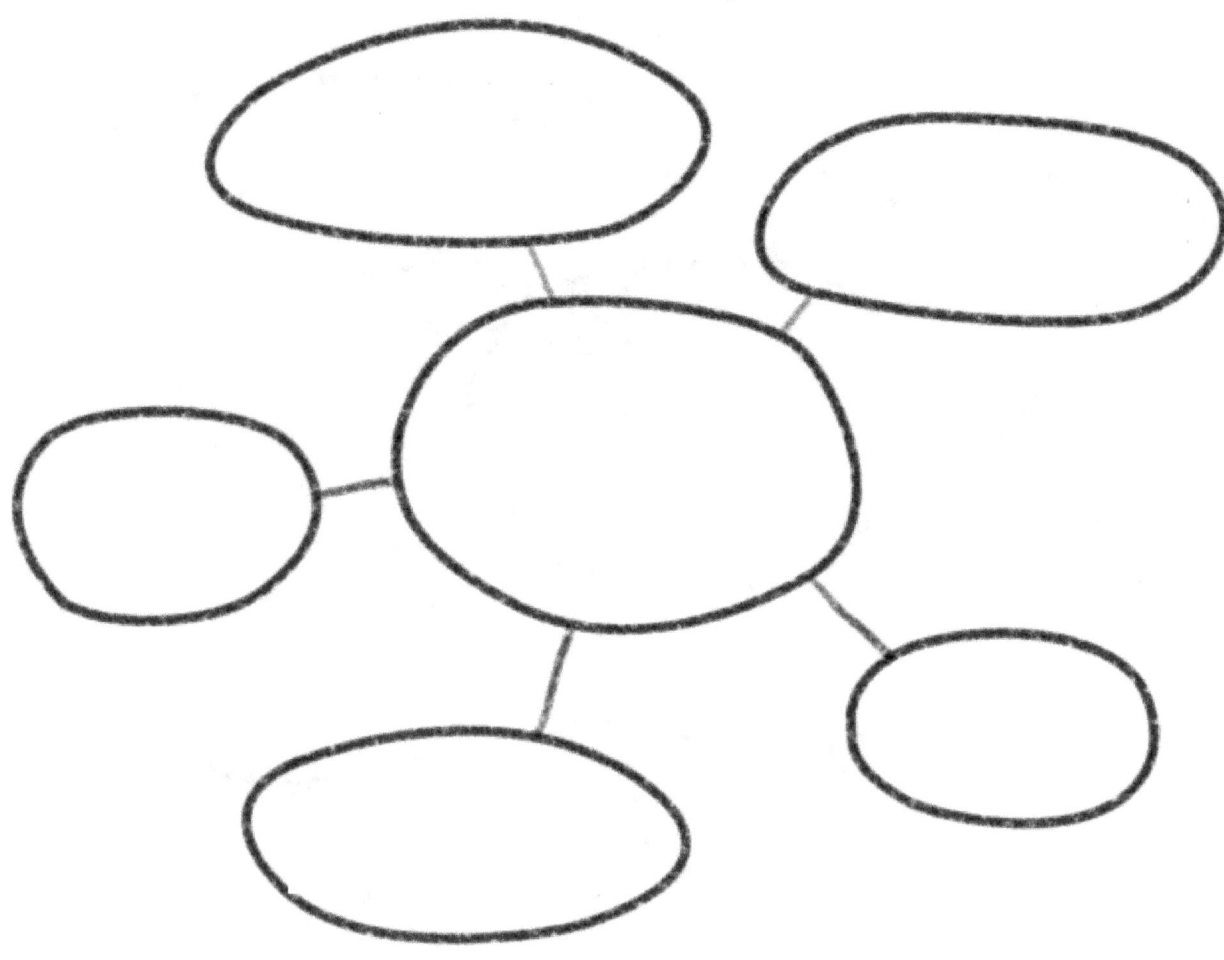

Diagram 2:

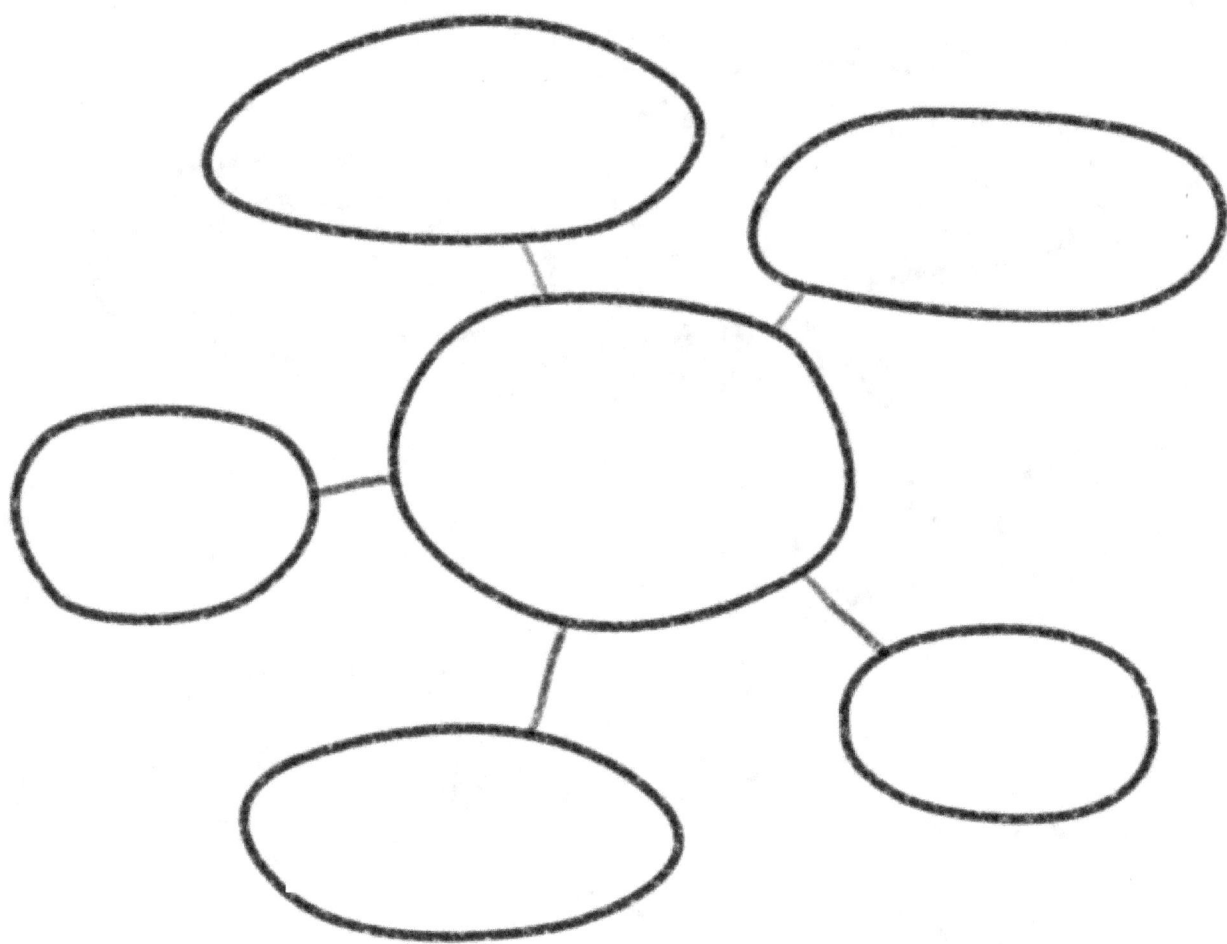

Diagram 3:

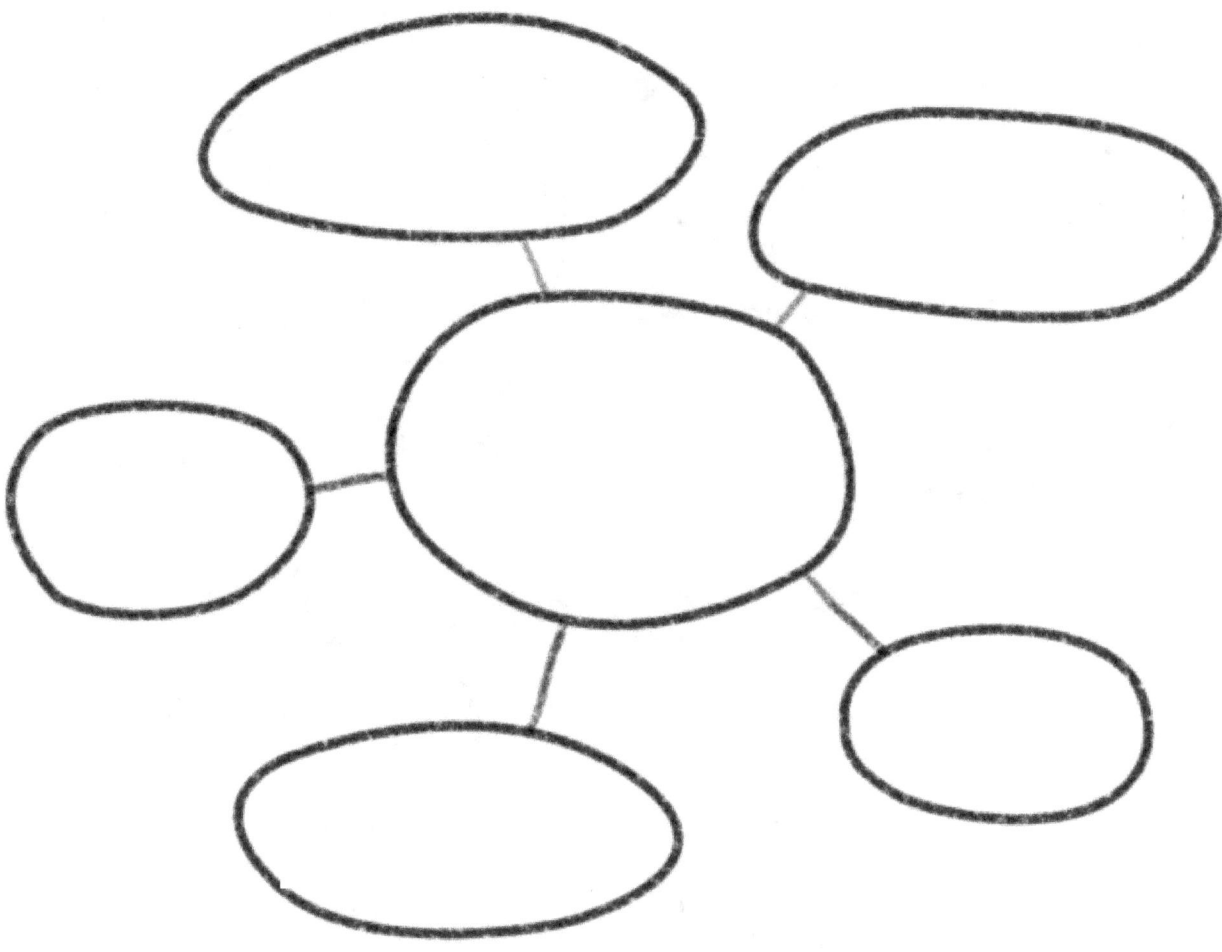

Diagram 4:

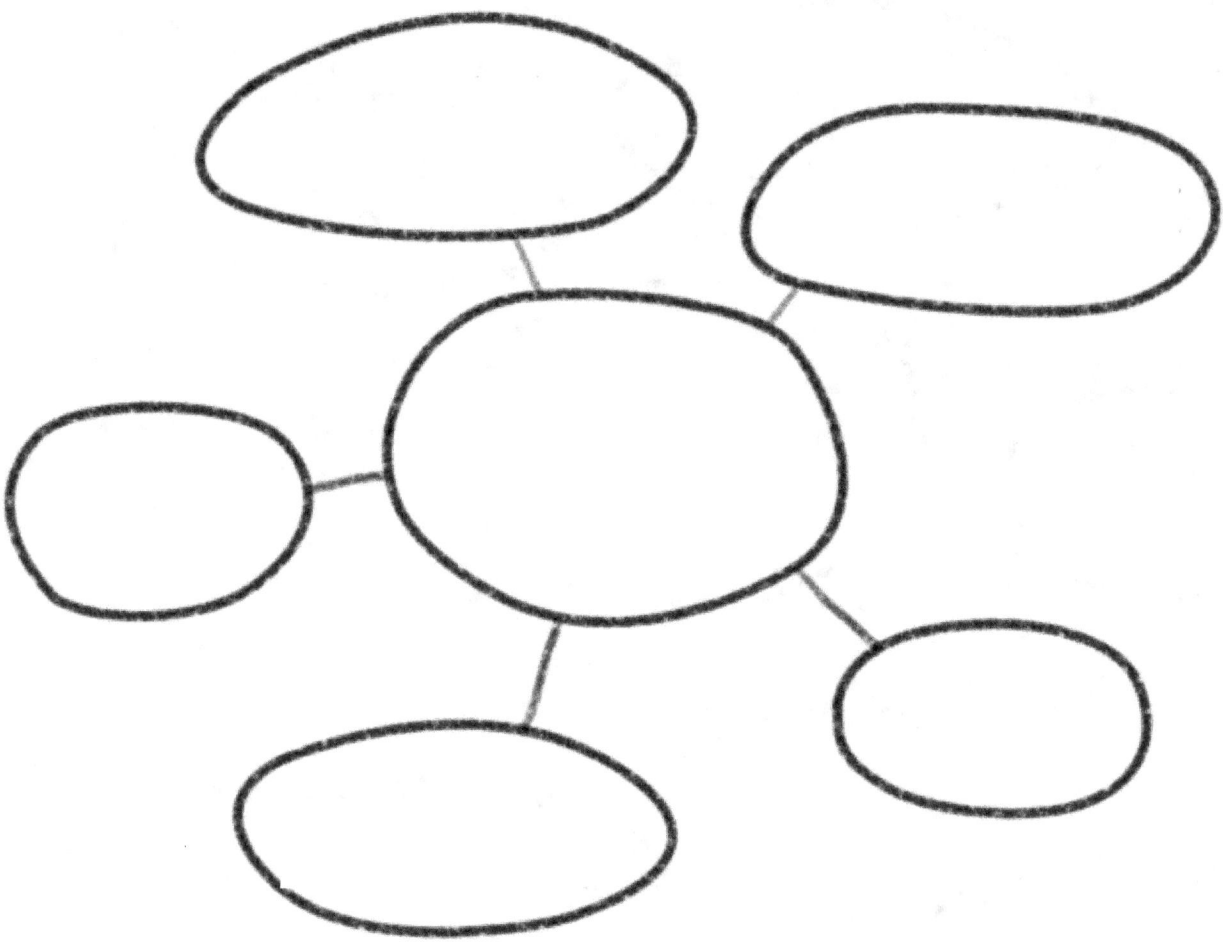

3.1.4 Written Exercise: Your Next 24 Blog Topics

Copy down the 24 blog post titles from your exercises above:

1. _____

2. _____

3. _____

4. _____

5. _____

6. _____

7. _____

8. _____

9. _____

10. _____

11. _____

12. _____

13. _____

14. _____

15. _____

16. _____

17. _____

18. _____

19. _____

20. _____

21. _____

22. _____

23. _____

24. _____

3.1.5 Action Step: Use Your Content Calendar

Once you have them all written down and organized, go to the **Bonus Blog and Social Media Content Calendar** (http://solvingthesocialmediapuzzle.com/calendar/) bonus you received and place topics on the calendar on the dates you will post them.

Lesson 4: Pick the Right Social Networks

Now that you have the WHO and WHY and a good start on your blog, it's time to figure out which network(s) you will commit to using over the next 60 days. We have outlined some "fast facts" on each network and how they are best used (from http://mashable.com/2012/04/16/social-networks-tips-infographic/).

Fast Facts: FACEBOOK

Information taken from an infographic published by OnlineMBA.com[i]

- **Largest of the social networks in terms of user base over 900k**
- **The average Facebook user has 130 friends**
- **The average Facebook visit lasts 23 minutes**
- **46% of Facebook users are over the age of 45**
- **57% of Facebook users are female (43% male)**
- **57% of Facebook users report having been to "some college" (24% bachelors or graduate degree)**
- **47% of Facebook users report making between $50,000 – $99,000 annually (33% between $25,000 – $49,999)**

Best Use:

For humanizing your brand, a coordinated, well-thought-out Facebook strategy can be a good choice. With the huge demographic segments that Facebook reaches, you're sure to have your business's sweet spot covered. Some people prefer to use

Facebook as a personal outlet, and formally separate their personal profile from their business page. Some prefer NOT to use a business page at all, but just use their personal profile to converse with friends and family as well as network with business people. It really is an individual choice that depends on your overall goals. However, daily conversation and reach-out is the best use of Facebook for business. Don't create a profile or page if you can't devote a significant amount of time to crafting updates and engaging people. Facebook ads work very well as an economical way to generate new audience with effective targeting. Photos, questions, video and fill-in-the-blank posts generate the most engagement and sharing.

Pros/Cons:

The biggest pro with Facebook is the huge audience and availability to leverage the "social graph" with ultra-targeted advertising. Also the built-in measurement and tracking ability with Facebook Insights lets you see exactly how well your posts are doing, so you can test and tweak easily. One of the biggest cons is the fact that the rules and/or interface seem to change frequently, which upsets users who don't like adjusting to new learning curves. Also, Facebook's Edgerank algorithm limits the visibility of most business posts to a fraction of the user's audience, making it challenging to gain traction.

4.1.1 Written Exercise - Answer these questions about Facebook:

- Does Facebook reach my targeted persona?

- Can Facebook help me reach my broadly defined objective?

- Can I dedicate at least 45 minutes per day to managing Facebook and interactions?

- Can I commit to posting at least 1 time every other day – with images and links?

If yes to all of these questions, Facebook may be the right network for you. Use the checklist in the addendum to get set up with Facebook.

Fast Facts: TWITTER

Statistics from OnlineMBA.com and Digital Surgeons [ii]

- **Twitter has 127 million users**
- **13% of Internet users also use Twitter**
- **54% of Twitter users use Twitter on their mobile devices**
- **36% of Twitter users tweet at least once a day**
- **The average visit on Twitter lasts for 11:50 minutes**
- **59% of Twitter users are female (41% male)**
- **Only 25% follow a brand**
- **Twitter generates over 250 million Tweets per day**

While it seems that Twitter has a large audience and lots of conversations going on, a 2009 Harvard study[iii] showed that:

- Only 21% of Twitter users are active users
- 34% of Twitter users hadn't tweeted even once
- A whopping 73% of Twitter's users tweeted less than ten times

You have to be a "power user" to get noticed on this network

Best Use:

Twitter is great for real-time customer interaction and conversation. We also recommend its use for brand recognition and building communities. Since you can follow up to 2,000 people without anyone following you back, you have a real tool to make connections quickly.

Pros/Cons

Twitter allows you to speak in real-time to your customers and interact with people in quick messages. It makes you think about how to be succinct in your communications. It is also a great place to connect with other influencers quickly but remember to be strategic and not just sell.

On the other hand, a Tweet is like a grain of sand in the ocean, put it out there and waves of other tweets come on top of it and wash it away. You must dedicate the time and effort that is necessary to get noticed and utilize twitter to its fullest potential. Do not just send one tweet a day and think you will get interactions. Over 71% of tweets get no interaction at all! That means you have to be committed to using this network – 5-10 tweets per day minimum

Also, remember that Twitter users can say anything about anyone they want, so make sure you are on top of any negative comments that are happening.

4.1.2 Written Exercise: Answer these questions about Twitter:

- Does Twitter reach my targeted persona? Yes/no

- Can Twitter help me reach my broadly defined objective?

- Can I dedicate at least 45 minutes per day to managing Twitter and interactions?

- Can I commit to posting at least five tweets per day (not including RT and Replies)

If yes to all of these questions, Twitter may be the right network for you. Use the checklist in the addendum to get set up with Twitter.

Fast Facts: LINKEDIN

Statistics from OnlineMBA.com:

- **LinkedIn has members in over 200 countries**
- **LinkedIn has about 150 million registered users**
- **About half of the members are outside the US**
- **Executives from all Fortune 500 companies are LinkedIn members**
- **Higher income levels (many over $100k per year)**
- **More than half have a higher education degree**
- **Demographic evenly split between male and female**
- **75% of LinkedIn users use it for business purposes**
- **There are 2 million companies represented on LinkedIn**

Nielsen Online says that the demographics of LinkedIn members compares to other major business outlets such as the *Wall Street Journal*, *Forbes* and *Businessweek*.

Best Use:

This is the network on which to be present for business-to-business services, and for reaching out to the C-suite executive. LinkedIn is most useful for lead generation because many people are on LinkedIn to do business. Answer (and ask) questions; this is an under-used but great way to discover what people are requesting information about. It's also a great platform for establishing yourself as an expert in your field and in doing so, gain brand awareness for you and your company.

Pros/Cons:

For people who are more comfortable with a closed network, without the distractions of fast-moving streams of conversation, LinkedIn can be a great tool. Its search capability gives it much strength, allowing users to find other people and research companies, look for and post jobs, and showcase expertise, all within one network. It does take time to get momentum going and to get found in search, but overall it's a good networking tool. Some complain about the stodgy profile interface and the inability to schedule posts on business profiles using automated schedulers. While business profiles allow a little more creativity in presentation (within limits), not being able to schedule updates there is a negative.

4.1.3 Written Exercise: Answer these questions about Linkedin

Does Linkedin reach my targeted persona? Yes/no

- Can Linkedin help me reach my broadly defined objective?

- Can I dedicate at least 45 minutes per day to managing Linkedin and interactions?

- Can I commit to posting at least 2 times per day into Groups, Answer 1 question per week?

If yes to all of these questions, Linkedin may be the right network for you. Use the checklist in the addendum to get set up with Linkedin.

Fast Facts: YOUTUBE

Statistics from YouTube.com iv

- **60 hours of video are uploaded every minute, or one hour of video is uploaded to YouTube every second**
- **Over 4 billion videos are viewed a day**
- **Over 800 million unique users visit YouTube each month**
- **Over 3 billion hours of video are watched each month on YouTube**
- **More video is uploaded to YouTube in one month than the 3 major US networks created in 60 years**
- **70% of YouTube traffic comes from outside the US**
- **YouTube is localized in 39 countries and across 54 languages**
- **In 2011, YouTube had more than 1 trillion views or almost 140 views for every person on Earth**
- **500 years of YouTube video are watched every day on Facebook, and over 700 YouTube videos are shared on Twitter each minute**
- **100 million people take a social action on YouTube (likes, shares, comments, etc) every week**

Best Use:

YouTube is the place to be for brand awareness and SEO. It is great for brand awareness because you can create how-to videos, promotional videos or video blogs on any topic. The more videos you post, the more likely they are to be seen by users who are either searching for that topic, or have viewed a similar video to yours (your video could show up in the list of other suggested videos)

Pros/Cons:

Setting up a channel is relatively easy, so getting started and building a profile is simple. The fact that Google favors video is another helpful plus, so with the right tagging and descriptions, your videos can gain traction quickly. YouTube is also good for cross-promotion and sharing of videos across other mediums, and its popularity makes it a powerful search engine. Not everyone is comfortable creating, producing and editing video, however. It's not as easy as writing an update, which makes it a little harder to use for the beginner—and there's a definite learning curve with equipment, lighting and editing software. However, those issues are not insurmountable—lots of videos are available to help beginners walk through the process!

4.1.4 Written Exercise: Answer these questions about YouTube:

- Does YouTube reach my targeted persona? Yes/no

- Can YouTube help me reach my broadly defined objective?

- Can I dedicate at least a few minutes per day to managing my YouTube channel and interactions?

- Can I commit to posting at least 1 new video a week?

If yes to all of these questions, YouTube may be the right network for you, use the checklist in the addendum to get set up with YouTube.

Fast Facts: GOOGLE PLUS (also Google + or G+)

Statistics from OnlineMBA.com and TheSocialSkinny.com

- **Google+ has had 90 million unique visitors**
- **More than 30% of those users are in the US**
- **Google+ users are 71% male**
- **The most common occupation of a Google+ user is an engineer**
- **44% of Google+ users are "single"**
- **The Google+ button is served more than five billion times a day**

What does this tell us? Although Google+ is a relatively new platform, its growth and integration in "all things Google" make it a powerful tool for business users, especially for SEO. The demographic is skewed more male (perhaps a bit more techy), but these are serious users who log in and share content regularly, with the lion's share being from the US.

Best Use: G+ is a great social network for people who have specific interests. Photographers, gardeners, business niche interests—all do well when they use G+ as a connection tool—not just a business platform. Having a personal profile (as opposed to just a business profile) and building circles is best, since personal profiles have more leeway to connect with other people freely. G+ is a very visual platform, too; photo/screenshot sharing is popular.

Pros/cons: People who like G+ say they appreciate the clean, open interface and lack of "noise," such as games, ads and other attention-shifters. With less noise, it's also easier to connect and converse with influencers on the platform. Being able to send different messages to different lists (or circles) is also helpful, and the program makes it easy to create and manipulate those lists with drag/drop functionality.

Live "Hangouts" are another nice feature that lets you chat with up to ten people simultaneously via video, share documents and spreadsheets. Hangouts are one of its more popular features. Then, of course, there's the SEO component. Getting your messages more Google oomph is a definite plus.

As for cons, here are a few that users have noted:

- As a social networking site, G+ has received less interest. Many still prefer Facebook and can't leave it easily.

- You need to have a Gmail account to set up a profile.

- No API—no way to manage your G+ account from a 3rd party application.

- G+ offers limited customization compared to Facebook.

- Many G+ users find it annoying that Google pushes posts with new comments back to the top of the timeline and consider it a drawback.

- The inability to gain traction with just a business page (must use a personal profile as well to reach out to people).

4.1.5 Written Exercise: Answer these questions about Google+:

- Does G+ reach my targeted persona? Yes/no
- Do you have a Gmail account?
- Am I comfortable having a G+ personal AND business page?
- Can G+ help me reach my broadly defined objective?
- Can I dedicate at least a few minutes per day to managing my G+ profile and interactions?
- Can I commit to posting and/or sharing updates and building circles at least 2-3 times a week?
- If yes to all of these questions, G+ may be the right network for you. Use the checklist in the addendum to get set up with G+.

4.1.6 Other Social Networks

Social media is an ever-changing landscape of marketing channels. Write down any others where your market may live and how you're going to use them.

_____

_____

_____

_____

_____

_____

Lesson Five: How Will You Engage?

As mentioned in **Step Five** of our book, you have a few choices for implementing an engagement strategy once your platforms are chosen. You can do it all yourself, hire in-house help, or outsource engagement. Below are some questions you need to answer before making this decision:

5.1.1 Action Step: Ask yourself some questions:

Can I realistically do this myself?

Are you willing to commit the time to learn the platform(s) etiquette and best practices?

Are you willing to commit the amount of time needed to adequately manage and engage on the platforms you've chosen?

Are you comfortable sharing with other people? You need to put a little of yourself out there—you can't hide behind a logo.

Are you willing to engage in real conversation (and not just sell)?

NOTE: If you answered "No" to any of the above questions, then attempting engagement on your own isn't advisable. Get some help from either internal or external resources, or you'll be frustrated with your results.

If you are going to outsource to a virtual assistant here are some questions to be sure to ask:

- Please list some past results you've achieved for other clients.
- How do you stay on top of the latest social media trends?
- What's your content syndication strategy/process?
- What kind of results have you achieved for your own business via social?

Be sure to check them out! Here are some red flags to watch out for:

- Don't have a strong following online (It's ok if they don't have 20,000 followers, but if they only have 30, then you know there's a problem).
- Don't have a blog that is updated regularly with good content.
- Only use one or two social networking sites for themselves.
- Thinks social media marketing is the only type of marketing you need.
- Promises great results quickly.
- You know more than they do about social media.

Whether you're doing this yourself, or handing it off to an employee or outsourcing, make sure you have written rules for engagement. Here's a link to a clearinghouse of Social Media Policies for various types of businesses: http://socialmediagovernance.com/policies.php.

5.1.2 Written Exercise: Characteristics and Interview Questions

Write down the characteristics of the person you will outsource your social media to and compile a list of interview questions:

Characteristics: Write down the top ten in order of importance

1. _____

2. _____

3. _____

4. _____

5. _____

6. _____

7. _____

8. _____

9. _____

10. _____

Interview questions: Ask questions that give you a good idea of the person's experience and results they've achieved for others. Examples could include: How long have you been using social media for your business? What types of businesses have you done this for? Which platforms do you have the most experience in? Can you show me some specifics on what you've achieved for other clients?

1. _____

2. _____

3. _____

4. _____

5. _____

6. _____

7. _____

8. _____

9. _____

10. _____

5.1.3 Written Exercise: Planning a listening campaign

In the book we talk about the importance of doing a listening campaign to find out what if anything people are saying and how they're saying it.

Look for five blogs in your niche, write them down in the space below and subscribe to them online. Do the same for profiles on Facebook, Twitter and any other profiles you've chosen to work with over the next 60 days. Study the types of posts created, and look for posts with lots of engagement (comments, likes, shares, etc.).

Blogs

1. _____

2. _____

3. _____

4. _____

5. _____

Social media platform chosen: _____

When viewing the comments and activity on each network, look for patterns such as:

✓ What kind of posts are they? (Informational, how-to, questions, etc.)
✓ What visuals were used (graphics/video)?
✓ What kinds of comments did they receive?

What is the content that gets most engagement and interaction?

_____

_____

_____

_____

_____

_____

5.1.4 Action Step: Set up and Run Google Alerts

Another way to place your "ear to the Internet" is to set up Google Alerts for your name, company name, competitor names and top three key phrases. Monitor your alerts and track mentions, so you know what's being said online. Change them as needed and review monthly.

Use this space to write down the keywords you will use to set up your Google Alerts:

_____

_____

_____

_____

_____

_____

_____

_____

5.1.5 Weekly Exercise: Trend Searches

Use Search.Twitter.com and/or Google Trends to get a snapshot of what's going on around your keywords/industry.

Use this space to write down the topics you will regularly search:

_____

_____

_____

_____

_____

_____

_____

_____

_____

_____

5.1.6 Written Exercise: Plan a Moderation Strategy

As we refer to in the book, it is important when you begin to be active on the networks that you are prepared for all types of feedback. Write out a list of the top 20 negative things customers have (or could) say about your product or service. Next to each comment, write out the optimal response. Involve your customer service and/or legal department here if you have one. Take some time to brainstorm helpful, positive replies to these comments, making sure to leave space for personalization.

Write out a list of positive comments and list your response style to each. Here is an example:

Client: Your product is terrible! It didn't do anything you said it could.

Response: We're sorry that you're having trouble, [NAME]. Please contact customer service at [800# or email] so that we can take care of this for you ASAP.

Client: I just LOVE your product! I use it all the time.

Response: Thank you [NAME]. It always makes us feel good if we can help make life a little easier for our friends.

Use this space and the space on the next page to write ten responses to positive comments and negative comments. You want a variety so the responses don't look "canned."

Responses to complaints:

1. _____
2. _____
3. _____
4. _____
5. _____
6. _____
7. _____
8. _____
9. _____
10. _____

Responses to compliments:

1. _____
2. _____
3. _____
4. _____
5. _____
6. _____

7. _____

8. _____

9. _____

10. _____

Lesson 6: Measuring results

6.1.1 Action Step: Set up a Google Analytics account

The key to measuring results is to get good tools to help you. You cannot possibly manually tabulate all of the information needed to create a successful online marketing strategy.

We recommend setting up a Google Analytics account for your website/blog, and take some time to learn how to view your website metrics and what affects them from external sources. Google has a great primer on how to use Analytics here: http://support.google.com/analytics/?hl=en.

6.1.2 Written Exercise: Write out your goals

Measurement begins with goal-setting. Decide what your top two or three goals for using each social media platform are (including your blog), and quantify those with dates by which you would like to achieve them. For example: Brand Awareness—Increase fans by 10% in 60 days (list date).

My Blog

TOP Goals:	% Change	by (Date)
1._____		
2._____		
3._____		

Facebook

TOP Goals:	% Change	by (Date)
1._____		
2._____		
3._____		

Twitter

TOP Goals:	% Change	by (Date)
1._____		
2._____		
3._____		

LinkedIn

TOP Goals:	% Change	by (Date)
1._____		
2._____		
3._____		

YouTube

TOP Goals:	% Change	by (Date)
1.		
2.		
3.		

Google +

TOP Goals:	% Change	by (Date)
1.		
2.		
3.		

(Other Platform)

TOP Goals:	% Change	by (Date)
1.		
2.		
3.		

6.1.3 Measuring Blog Effectiveness:

How do you know if your blog efforts are successful? While the answer to that question depends on the goals you have set, there are certain numbers to pay attention to, starting with the number of people who subscribe to your blog. Subscription programs like feedburner.com help you keep track of your subscriber numbers, but you'll want to go a bit deeper to track the effectiveness of your content. Here are some top metrics to track:

Visits and unique visitors: How are people finding your site, and where are they coming from? Where do they go on your site once they're there?

Page views; look at specific pages and what readers do there: Which pages get the most traffic? How long do people stay? How do people click around on your site, and what links are they using?

Comments: Are readers interacting with your blog? If not, then either your blog isn't getting seen by enough people, or the content doesn't resonate well enough.

Social media shares: Count social media shares and note which platforms readers use (such as Facebook, Twitter, LinkedIn and others like StumbleUpon).

Video or other media downloads or views: Are people downloading your content or viewing your videos?

Much of this can be tracked using Google Analytics, however, there are dashboards like CLICKY which incorporate analytics into your blog and allow easier viewing of results.

6.1.4 Action Step: Research analytics programs

Do some Google research on dashboard analytics programs for websites and blogs. You may have to do a few free trials to see which interface you like best.

Write your top 3 picks here:

1st Choice: _____

2nd Choice: _____

3rd Choice: _____

6.1.5 Action Step: Make Analytics a Habit

Make a weekly appointment in your content calendar for reviewing Google Analytics and/or an alternative dashboard.

Mark your calendar to spend a few minutes each month to review these metrics in light of the goals you set earlier. Keep those appointments!

6.1.6 Measuring Facebook

Having healthy fan growth is certainly important, but even more important is measuring your Facebook post effectiveness. We have found that it's optimal to budget some Facebook advertising to help build a quality fan base, and concentrate on posting valuable content for a while first. It can take a while to build engagement, so be patient, and willing to try a varied approach to posting to get a feel for what your audience likes. You should get used to using Facebook Insights and paying attention to patterns.

Study Facebook Insights

Take a few moments to familiarize yourself with the Facebook Insights tool. Use the "Help" menu to find Facebook-provided information on it, and when you get into the dashboard, click on the "?" links for the definitions of each term. In particular, pay attention to LIKES, REACH and TALKING ABOUT THIS, rather than concentrating purely on number of fans.

Again, make an appointment in your calendar to review Insights on a weekly, bi-weekly and/or monthly basis, so you can get an idea of how people are interacting with your posts.

For deeper insights, check out these free dashboard tools from Simply Measured at http://simplymeasured.com/free-social-media-tools#/. You can spend lots of money on dashboards and measurement tools, but we recommend getting as much as you can out of Facebook's Insights first.

6.1.7 Written Exercise: Who's Writing on Your Wall?

Open your Facebook Page and view your wall. Scan your posts and segment them into types (video, link share, photo, text, poll, etc.). Then look for how many times each post was liked, commented on and shared. Add the time of the post, and write this information down on the lines below (example listed first):

Short Post Title	Type	Time	Likes,	Comments,	Shares
Favorite color	Question	3PM	2	1	0

_____

_____

_____

_____

_____

_____

_____

_____

Other ways to measure engagement:

How many of your fans posted on your wall this week?

Were they positive, negative or spammy in nature?

Did you receive any private messages from fans?

Do this in conjunction with looking at Insights to see what patterns emerge. You may get more interaction at certain times of day, with certain types of posts, and you can use this data to tweak your posting approach.

6.1.8 Measuring Twitter

As with Facebook, counting the number of followers isn't the only measure of how well you're doing with Twitter.

You do need to pay attention to follower growth over time, however. By tracking the number of your Twitter followers and net new followers, you can get a sense of the growth of your Twitter reach monthly. Here's an example. For computing your following growth in July, you would pull the numbers from June and July and use this formula:

(July Twitter Followers - June Twitter Followers) / June Twitter Followers = Growth %

Tracking this percentage every month allows you to see whether your tweeting strategies are helping to increase your reach. You can also use tools like Twitter Counter to see a dashboard of your growth (Twitter Counter has both free and paid versions).

Other items to pay attention to are **Re-tweets (RTs)** and **@mentions**, which indicate the level of engagement with your posts. If you use a scheduler dashboard like Hootsuite, it's easy to see these at a glance, but you can also view them in your Twitter profile. If your content is resonating with your audience, you'll see more and more RTs and @mentions. For more overall statistics on how your tweets are performing, try an inexpensive analysis dashboard tool like Sprout Social (you can get a free trial).

6.1.9 Written Exercise:

Take a look at your Twitter feed for the past week, and write down your:

✓ **Top re-tweeted post:** _____

What time of day did you tweet it? How many RT's did it get? What was the subject? Who re-tweeted it? Was it sharing someone else's content or your own?

✓ **Number of @mentions:** _____

Same questions as above

6.2.1 LinkedIn Metrics

Easy numbers to track on LinkedIn are the number of times your profile has been viewed, and the number of times you've shown up in search. You can view this on your home page, and it looks like this:

Who's Viewed Your Profile?

6 Your profile has been viewed by 6 people in the past 15 days.

22 You have shown up in search results 22 times in the past 7 days.

But the real indicator of how well you're doing on LinkedIn is the amount of feedback you get from your networking efforts and updates. Keep track of Likes, Shares and Comments on your updates, and reach out immediately to thank people who respond.

6.2.2 Action Step: Track Mentions of Your Name using LinkedIn Signal

Search for your name or company name in LinkedIn Signal Keyword Mentions. At the top of your profile next to the search box, click the dropdown menu for Updates, and enter your name. Save the search, and do another one for your company name and another for your industry or a keyword (example below). Check these periodically by clicking on Saved Search.

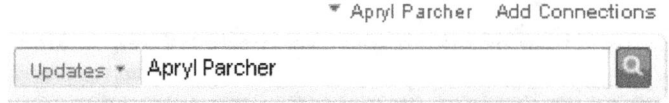

6.2.3 Action Step: Track Likes and Comments

Click on your "Profile," and then "View Profile" from the navigation pane at the top of your LinkedIn page. In your latest update, click on "See all Activity," to view how people have responded to your posts.

6.2.4 Action Step: Track "Expert" Designation in Answers

Have you been asking and answering questions in LinkedIn? When your answers receive "Best Answer" designation enough times, you receive an expert designation in that category. To view your expert status, "View" your profile and scroll down to your Q&A section in the right column, just above recommendations. Make it a priority to answer at least one or two questions a week where you can contribute valuable insights to gain recognition as an expert.

6.2.5 Measuring YouTube

YouTube has an easy analytics dashboard so you can track how well your channel and videos are doing. If you haven't played around with it yet, do so. Access it from "My Channel" right next to "Video Manager" (see the image below).

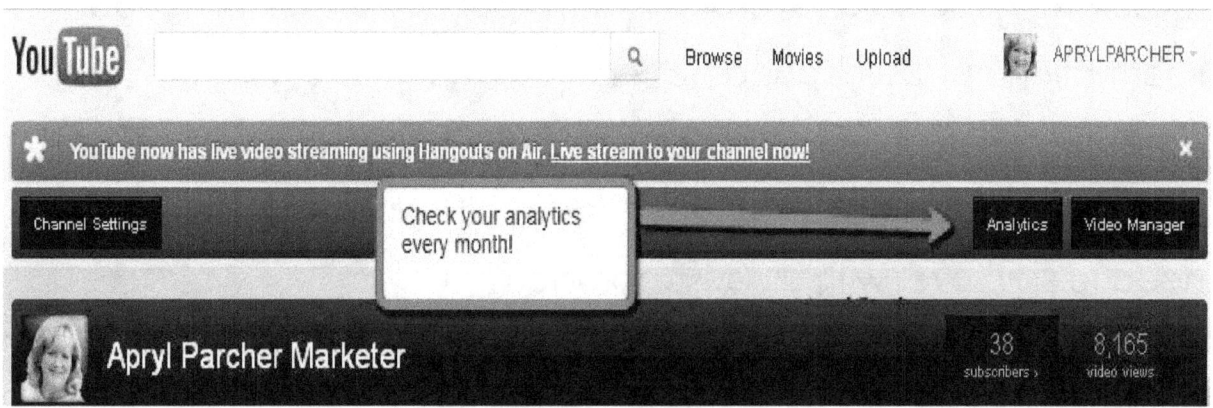

6.2.6 Written Exercise: Analyze Most Popular Videos

Open your YouTube Analytics Dashboard and write down the information on your top 2 performing videos in the space below. Based on this information, think of two new video ideas where you could replicate success.

Video Title	Views	Likes	Shares	Comments

6.2.7 Written Exercise: Analyze Poorest Performing Videos

In the space below, write down the titles of your poorest performing videos (those with no or few views, no likes or comments. Now think like your main persona might when looking at this video title. Comparing them to your most popular videos, try to think of the top reason why each didn't resonate with your audience. Is it good information but just needs a better title? Is it too salesy? Is the topic not important to your target audience? Be honest with yourself in this evaluation. Can you salvage this video with some editing or do you need to start over with a new approach?

Video Title   **Top Negative**   **Salvage/Abandon**

_____

_____

_____

_____

6.2.8 Measuring G+

As with any other social platform, level of engagement is what you need to track on G+, which includes comments, shares and 1+s. It's a good idea to keep track of are the people who are actively sharing your stuff, because they are your "message amplifiers" that can help you spread the word quickly about new initiatives and launches. This is an idea shared by Christopher S. Penn on his *Awaken Your Super Hero* blog. Put those people in a special circle and reach out to them to thank them and network, and to build collaborative, sharing relationships.

6.2.9 Action Step: Sift Your Stream for Amplifiers and Circle Them

Find the shares at the bottom of your Google+ posts; click the pictures to open the activity dialog box. Then hover over each name and add them to a circle of amplifiers.

Write down the names of your top Amplifiers in the space below, look up any other social profiles and websites, and reach out to them.

_____

_____

_____

_____

If you're looking to see how your G+ activity stacks up in traffic to your website, Google Analytics is the place to go. There is a nice dashboard feature within Analytics for social media reporting, which you can use to see at a glance which platforms drove traffic to your website, and how they travelled through it.

Lesson 7: Putting it all together

Now that you've gone through the book and exercises, it's time to get going on your social media plan. Write down all the information from the exercises above and start to implement.

7.1.1 Written Exercise:

My target persona is: _____

My Goal is: _____

My targeted network is; _____

My main source(s) of analyzing performance: _____

_____

_____

_____

_____

_____

7.1.2 Action Step: Print out materials

Print out the persona you are focusing on, the goal(s), your blog post topics, and learn the targeted network inside and out. Be sure to measure your performance and now **GET TO WORK!**

Stay the course for the next 60 days and let us know how you're doing by sending us an email at:
http://solvingthesocialmediapuzzle.com/feedback/.

Addendum

Checklists and Suggested Activity for Social Networks:

Facebook Checklist for Success:

Create your Daily Activity Facebook Plan.

Most people are like you; too busy to dedicate several hours per day to Facebook. But in order to create a good presence and strong connections, you will have to schedule some Facebook time every day.

☐ Every morning set aside about 15-20 minutes to have a cup of coffee/tea with Facebook. You will find it is a great way to start your day. Scheduling another 15-20 minutes in the evening or late afternoon to check in and interact will help you grow your community. Once you create this routine, you will enjoy spending quality time with your friends and fans.

☐ Create a list of on-going topics to discuss or post. This is an organic list that will change as you learn what your fans want. Your community will get to know you better when you establish consistency and deliver value.

☐ Example list:

   o Give an expert tip.

   o Share something you've learned (mention the source/give credit/share a link), or ask a question about your community and their needs.

o Ask or tell about events in your industry (local, live or virtual).

o Share your personal interests or passions. (affirmation, motivational quote, an anecdote)

Suggested Facebook Activities:

Remember our 3x15 plan? Use this schedule as a guide to planning your Facebook activities each day.

Morning Facebook activity:

Schedule (15 min):

- ✓ Check birthdays, post happy birthday messages on friend's wall(s).

- ✓ Check your Wall for any posts by friends and reply to any you see relevant and interesting.

- ✓ Connect with at least 4-5 people and comment on their posts.

- ✓ Create your morning post, whether it is a tip, an inspirational quote, or a link to some interesting content you want to share.

- ✓ Check your Fan Page for activity and reply to comments posted by Fans.

- ✓ Update your Page status (check your Topics List for ideas).

Mid-day/evening Facebook activity

Schedule (15 min each):

- ✓ Check your Wall for any posts by friends and reply to any you see relevant and interesting.

✓ Connect with at least 4-5 people and comment on their posts.

✓ Create your mid-day/evening post, whether it is a tip, an inspirational quote, or a link to some interesting content you want to share (different from the morning post).

✓ Check your Fan Page for activity and reply to comments posted by Fans.

✓ Search for pages you may be interested in and become a fan of at least one.

✓ Engage in conversation on two of your favorite pages.

Update your Page status (check your Topics List for ideas).

Twitter Checklist for Success:

☐ Create your Daily Activity Twitter Plan

Most people are like you, too busy to dedicate several hours per day to Twitter. But in order to create a branded presence and valuable connections, you will have to schedule Twitter time every day.

Schedule time

o Every morning set about 15 minutes to have a cup of coffee/tea with Twitter. You will find it is a great way to start your day. Scheduling another 15 minutes at the end of your work day or in the evening to check in and engage with your followers will help you grow your network.

Plan the types of Tweets

o Create a list of on-going topics to tweet about

o Follow this model to create a variety of different tweets

Tweet Types:

Information: Share your expertise or give your followers links to great articles by industry leaders.

Facebook Change Alert: Facebook is now allowing any administrator to remove any other administrator. Previously the... http://bit.ly/99yGID
12:48 PM Jun 14th via Facebook

Re-Tweet: Pass on something you've learned about from a fellow tweeter by putting RT before their username. Be sure to give credit to the source.

RT @mashable The iPhone 4 Is Here http://bit.ly/c1X7MX
#apple #iphone #iphone-4g
11:44 AM Jun 8th via TweetMeme

Question: Ask your following a question to promote a discussion.

What one thing would you make sure you had for a 2.5 hr
daily commute besides cell & computer?
7:52 AM Jun 21st via Power Twitter

Share: Talk about events in your industry (local, live or virtual). If you're attending an event, Tweet info about the event live from the venue.

katkrose Kathryn Rose
So excited! My new book The Parent's Guide to Facebook is out.
Parents-do U know what UR children are doing online? http://ow.ly
/2TCDw
1 hour ago

Inspiration: Share something about your personal interests or passions such as an affirmation, motivational quote or tip.

Tomorrow can be exactly the same as today if you keep doing
exactly what you're doing right now OR you can...
http://fb.me/AbJXwAeu
9:21 AM Jun 22nd via Facebook

Quotes: subscribe to daily quote emails, this is a great way to get inspirational, historical and other quotes to share with your Twitter followers.

Suggested Daily Twitter Activity Schedule

Morning Twitter Activities

- *5 min:*
  - ✓ Review current timeline of incoming tweets to check what your community is talking about
  - ✓ Respond to any DM's
  - ✓ Check your @replies and respond to any questions or comments
  - ✓ Re-Tweet one of your followers
  - ✓ Post one new original tweet
- *10 min:*
  - ✓ Check your Google Reader for articles of interest to your followers and choose at least one to share.
  - ✓ Check your tweet types list and create 3-5 additional new tweets to schedule.
- *5 min:*
  - ✓ Schedule those tweets using TweetDeck or Hootsuite. Space them out throughout the day, for example: 7:00am, 9:30am, 11:30am, 3:00pm, and 7:00pm.

Evening Twitter Activities

- ✓ *5-10 min:*
- ✓ Check out your new followers and chose whether to follow them back. Send them a personal welcome DM addressing them by their first name, and asking them a question (ex: *D Katkrose, kat, any great tips on soc media?*
- ✓ *1 min:* Check your DMs and reply to any if needed.
- ✓ *1 min:* Check your @replies and thank people for RT's, give kudos, or mentions.
- ✓ *5 min:* Review current timeline of incoming tweets and find some to engage with: RT, answer question, give kudos.
- ✓ *3 min:* Post couple of personal tweets: something funny that happened today or motivational quote.

Set a timer to help you stick to your schedule. You may find you need a bit more time in the beginning until you become confident in creating quality Tweets. But remember, Twitter is just one tool in your marketing strategy. Make Twitter work for you, not the other way around.

LinkedIn Checklist for Success

Here is an easy to follow checklist that will help you get on the right path and help you get the most out of LinkedIn.

Optimize your profile with Keyword rich:

- o Titles

- o Job Descriptions

- o Company summary

- ☐ Be sure to include your website links – using the "other" category and include keyword rich description of the link.

  - o Link to your blog, Facebook and any other pages that are relevant to you or your profession.

- ☐ Add your Twitter ID

- ☐ Assign a custom URL to make it easier to add to your website, email signature, etc.

- ☐ Search and ask for connections from people you know FIRST.

- ☐ Add the following applications:

  - o Slideshare

  - o Company Buzz/Twitter

  - o Events

  - o Blog Link or WordPress

  - o Reading List for Amazon

☐ Go to LinkedIn at least once per week and add something under the "What are you working on" area to keep your connections updated on you or your company's activities.

☐ Search for relevant, active groups and join them. Make sure you engage by:

   o Asking relevant questions

   o Provide good and relevant content

   o Asking for connections with other members

☐ At least once per week write a recommendation for another person and ask for a recommendation from others.

☐ Go into the "Answers" area regularly and search for questions where you can provide expertise.

Suggested Daily LinkedIn Activity Schedule:

   o   *5 min:*
      ✓ Review LinkedIn messages for items that need response.
      ✓ Review notifications and accept invitations to connect.
      ✓ Check your business page and post an update (personal profile can be checked and post scheduled in Hootsuite if you use that tool).

   o *10 min:*
      ✓ Check your Google Reader for articles of interest to your followers and choose at least one to share.

     ✓ Choose one group to post an update to.

    o *5 min:*

       ✓ Schedule any new updates to personal profile using Hootsuite.

Suggested Weekly LinkedIn Activity:

✓ *5-10 min:*

✓ Check out your new connections and see if they have followers you would like to connect to. Ask for introduction or see if they share any groups in common with you so you can send them a direct invitation to connect. Be sure to put a personal note in the invitation with a reason why you would like to connect (we belong to the same group, know this person, share an interest, etc.).

✓ Check your connections and choose one for making a recommendation. Reach out to that person to tell them you would like to recommend them, and ask them which business activity they would like you to make it under (personal or business profile, and category).

✓ Check your Q&A, and rate any answers that have come in for your questions.

20 min:

✓ Look for Questions in business categories in which you have expertise and pick one to answer where you can add value. Make it a thoughtful post, with links and helpful bullet points.

✓ Browse group posts and look for posts you can add a comment to.

✓ Add any new skills or expertise to your summary.

✓ Add to your reading list as appropriate.

YouTube Checklist for Success:

☐ Make sure when naming your channel, that you keep your name consistent with your website and other social network branding.

☐ Have a designer create a branded YouTube "Skin" that's consistent with your brand colors and images, and makes the best use of the available space.

☐ Maximize the space on your Profile with keywords.

☐ Link your Twitter and Facebook accounts (you can do this when editing settings under "Sharing").

☐ Be sure to adjust your settings for your desired privacy, emails, subscriptions and other preferences.

☐ When you create playlists, be strategic and use your keywords in the titles.

Think about creating videos in "sets" when you're camera ready, rather than one at a time, and consider setting up a specific spot in your office where you will always record. Set up your "studio" so that seating, background, lighting and tripod already set up and ready to go.

Write a brief script, and practice—make sure each video is under two minutes. Make sure your call to action is in the first ten seconds.

Write the title, URL, description and tags in a word document so it can be easily cut and pasted when you upload the video.

Engage with your viewers. Ask them to rate your existing videos and give you suggestions on future creations.

Don't forget to ask them to engage with you on other social networks!

Suggested Weekly YouTube Activity:

- ✓ Make a list of videos and include topics such as how-to, lists and tips that you think would be of interest your audience.
- ✓ Look for one or two videos to share in your "playlists."
- ✓ Check news sites and feeds to see if there are any relevant news stories circulating that you could use to add additional comments or content to create a new video post.
- ✓ Search for videos you may find interesting and "favorite" those by clicking the little red heart near the video.
- ✓ Make sure your videos are uploaded to your other social networking accounts and to your blog.
- ✓ Look at your page to see if there are new subscribers or comments. If someone comments on your video, make sure you reply to their comment; thank them for viewing your video and contributing to the value by communicating with you.

Google+ Checklist for Success:

(From our friend Elaine Lindsay at Trool Social Media http://troolsocial.com)

☐ Make sure your business page name is consistent with your website/blog and other social network branding.

☐ Maximize your keyword use through the info on your page.

☐ When you create photos, be strategic and use your keywords in the names.

☐ Link your social media accounts like Twitter, LinkedIn and Facebook in the 3 sections on your about tab.

☐ Get your Google+ Badges, both personal and business page to add to your website/blog.

☐ Be sure to set up your Authorship info for your website/blog.

☐ Be sure to adjust your settings for your desired privacy, emails, subscriptions, notifications and other preferences.

Daily Tasks for Google+

✓ Check your circles for engagement - respond to comments.

✓ Look for new notifications or check your circles for new people to circle back.

✓ When someone comments on your post, make sure you reply .

✓ Add commenter's to your circles.

✓ At minimum be sure to post Publicly at least once a day both personal and business page(s).

- ✓ Check news sites and feeds for relevant stories to create a new post.
- ✓ Search for photos and videos for you to share in your stream.
- ✓ Syndicate your posts to your other social networking accounts and to your website/blog.
- ✓ Join or start a Hangout to build more circles from the new people you meet.

Endnotes

[i] OnlineMBA. (2012). Infographic: A Case Study in Social Media Demographics, http://www.onlinemba.com/blog/social-media-demographics/

[ii] Digital Surgeons Facebook vs. Twitter Infographic http://www.digitalsurgeons.com/facebook-vs-twitter-infographic/

[iii] Harvard Business Review. (2009). Men Follow Men and Nobody Tweets, http://blogs.hbr.org/cs/2009/06/new_twitter_research_men _follo.html

[iv] YouTube statistics: http://www.youtube.com/t/press_statistics

www.ingramcontent.com/pod-product-compliance
Lightning Source LLC
Chambersburg PA
CBHW081505170526
45166CB00008B/2563